THE HIVE DETECTIVES

Chronicle of a Honey Bee Catastrophe

THE HIVE DETECTIVES

Chronicle of a Honey Bee Catastrophe

• Loree Griffin Burns •

with photographs by Ellen Harasimowicz

sandpiper

Houghton Mifflin Harcourt
Boston   New York

To my sister, Karin

Mary Duane heads out to inspect her backyard beehives.

RIGHT: A honey bee visits an apple blossom.

*Put on your veil, grab your hive tool,
and light up your smoker . . .*

. . . we're going into a beehive.

Before we begin, remember this: Honey bees are gentle insects.

Gentle? you ask. *But don't they have giant stingers on their rear ends?*

Well, yes, most bees do have a stinger at the tip of the abdomen. But they only use it in emergencies. If you move slowly and deliberately (no jerks in the bee yard!) and remember not to block the hive entrance (bees hate to find a strange body between them and the entrance to their hive), you can spend an enjoyable afternoon with thousands of honey bees and walk away without a single sting. Mary Duane does it all the time.

Mary is a hobbyist beekeeper. She keeps a small number of honey bee hives in her backyard for the pleasure of working with the bees and, of course, for the honey. Every week or two, from early spring until fall, Mary opens and inspects each of her hives to be sure the family of bees inside is healthy and safe. If anything is wrong with the colony—and, unfortunately, there are many things that can go wrong—Mary will see signs during the inspection. Her goal as beekeeper is to recognize these signs and take the steps needed to correct them. It's not an easy hobby, but the rewards, according to Mary, are many.

"When you work with bees you have to pay close attention to what you are doing," says Mary. "Everything else in your life drops away. The bees are fascinating, they help the environment, and the honey is great, but mostly I love that keeping bees forces me to be mindful."

In nearly ten years of beekeeping, Mary has been stung about twenty times—not bad when you consider she's handled *millions* of bees. Most of those stings happened early on, when Mary was new to working with honey bees. Now that she is used to the sights and sounds of an apiary, or bee yard, Mary is more relaxed and stings are rare. She wears a veil, of course, to protect her face, and she keeps sting remedies in her bee box, but she works her bees barehanded.

"I started off wearing gloves, but I find that I'm more gentle without them," Mary says. She pats the top of her bee box and adds, "If I come across an ornery hive, then I put my gloves on like anybody else."

Mary also keeps a smoker handy. Any worries the bees have about Mary poking through their home—worries they communicate with each other by releasing a smelly chemical called alarm pheromone—will be masked by the smell of smoke. Unable to smell alarm pheromone, the majority of bees in the hive don't realize anything is amiss and, as a result, remain calm during the inspection.

To prepare the smoker, Mary fills it with dry pine needles, drops in a lit match, and fans the flames with air from an attached bellows. Once the needles are burning well she closes the top and a thin line of smoke issues from the metal spout.

Like most modern beehives, Mary's consist of several boxes, called supers, stacked one atop the other in a tower-like structure. The supers come in differ-

ent depths—and depending on the beekeeper, in different colors, too—but inside, all supers are the same: ten rectangular frames hang side by side.

Each frame provides a foundation on which the bees can build their wax honeycomb. They fashion rows and rows of hexagonal cells that will eventually be used to store food and raise young bees. Supers and frames are designed so that the honeycomb is arranged just as it would be in a wild hive. Of course, the removable frames and stackable supers make handling a man-made hive much easier than handling a wild hive in a hollow tree.

ABOVE LEFT: **Mary prepares her smoker.**

ABOVE RIGHT: **Mary keeps a box of tools, a pair of gloves, and a lit smoker nearby whenever she works her bees.**

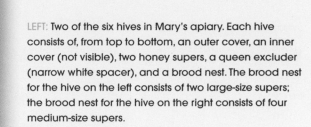

LEFT: Two of the six hives in Mary's apiary. Each hive consists of, from top to bottom, an outer cover, an inner cover (not visible), two honey supers, a queen excluder (narrow white spacer), and a brood nest. The brood nest for the hive on the left consists of two large-size supers; the brood nest for the hive on the right consists of four medium-size supers.

LEFT AND RIGHT: Each super contains ten two-sided sheets of honeycomb inside rectangular wooden frames. When the frames are hung side by side in the super (right), they form a structure similar to that of a wild honey bee hive (left). Wild hives are typically built in protected places—such as the hollow part of a tree—but this one was built on the side of a home in Wisconsin.

Mary begins her inspection at the top of a hive and works her way down. Because her hive tower is fitted with a queen excluder—a metal screen with openings large enough for worker bees but too small for a queen bee to squeeze through—the contents of each super is predictable. Above the queen excluder, in the part of the hive the queen can't reach, are the so-called honey supers. These will be full of worker bees storing nectar and turning it into honey. Below the queen excluder, toward the bottom of the hive, are the brood boxes. These are the only supers the queen has access to, and so they contain the result of her hard work: the colony's young and developing bees. Since developing bees are called brood, this part of the hive is often called the brood nest.

To get started, Mary grabs what looks like a small metal crowbar—beekeepers call it a hive tool—and pries open the first honey super.

"We beekeepers like to say that whoever invented the hive tool should get a Nobel Prize," Mary jokes as she works the hive tool into position. "It's that useful."

Hive tools are necessary because bees seal every crack and crevice in the hive with propolis, a gummy substance they make from the sap of plants and trees. Propolis protects the bees by keeping wind, water, and pests (such as ants and spiders) out of the hive, but it is a hassle for beekeepers.

"It's sticky!" says Mary. "There has never been a hive I couldn't open, but sometimes it takes a bit of muscle."

When she finally opens the top honey super and pulls out a frame, the news is good.

"Look at all that honey," she exclaims, pointing at the rippled wax surface the bees are crawling over. The bees made the wax and used it to cover, or cap, honey-filled comb cells. Though most cells on this first frame are capped, others are open,

BELOW: Some beekeepers collect propolis—the brownish gummy substance shown here—and use it to make medicinal creams.

BELOW: This frame is almost completely full of capped honey.

and sunlight bounces off the liquid nectar inside them. The bees collected this nectar from flowers in and around Mary's yard. When it is fully ripened into honey—a process that involves a little bee spit and a lot of evaporation—the bees will cap it, too. Eventually they will fill every cell on every frame of this super with honey. Only then will Mary collect and bottle it.

When she is satisfied with her inspection of the first honey super, Mary removes the entire box from the top of the hive tower and sets it gently on the ground. Then she begins to inspect the honey super below it. When this box also passes inspection, Mary is ready to move deeper into the hive. She pries off the queen excluder and takes her first look inside the brood nest.

RIGHT: In this close-up view of a honey frame you can see capped honey (top) and open cells of not-quite-finished honey. Worker bees fan the open cells with their wings until the nectar inside is highly concentrated, at which point they cover it with wax and save it for future use.

"This one is just boiling with bees!" she exclaims.

She blows smoke gently across the top of the box and then, just as she did in the honey supers, removes a single frame. Thousands of honey bees come with it, but Mary hardly notices them. Believe it or not, the bees hardly notice her either.

"This is beautiful," she says, gazing at the frame through her veil. "Perfect. I couldn't be happier. There's a great brood pattern."

She points beneath the crawling bees to an area of honeycomb covered with what looks like a graham cracker crust. The crust is actually more wax. Unlike the fresh wax that covers cells in the honey supers, the wax in the brood nest is recycled. It is darker in color and drier in appearance. In the brood nest, the wax-capped cells contain young bees in the final stages of their development. When the bee in each cell is fully developed, it will chew through the wax and join the hive.

LEFT: These wax-covered cells contain brood, or developing bees. The empty cells have been cleaned and are ready for new eggs; the irregular hole in this image was created by an emerging worker bee as she chewed her way out of her cell.

ABOVE: The majority of a hive's bees are found in the brood nest, where developing bees are cared for. Compare the number of bees on this brood frame to the number of bees on the honey frame Mary is holding in the photo on page 5.

7

Eggs, larvae, and capped brood are all signs that this colony's queen is healthy. Although Mary doesn't see the queen herself—she is lost among the thousands and thousands of bees in the brood nest—the presence of young larvae prove she is here, somewhere.

"She's doing a nice job," Mary says thoughtfully as she continues to study the brood nest.

In addition to developing bees, Mary finds capped honey, nectar, and pollen in the brood nest. Worker bees use these stores to feed themselves and the growing larvae. Mary examines each frame for signs of disease (thankfully, there are none) and for signs that the colony might soon swarm, or split into two separate colonies. Although swarming is a normal and healthy activity in the beehive, it limits honey production. Most beekeepers work hard to prevent it, and Mary is pleased to find no signs of swarming today.

When the inspection is finished, Mary rebuilds the hive frame by frame and

ABOVE: Beekeepers keep careful records of their hive activities in order to better manage their bee colonies throughout the year.

"And here are some larvae," Mary adds, pointing out a few open cells, each housing a curled white grub. Eventually, when these larvae grow big enough, their cells will be capped and they, too, will begin the process of transforming into adult bees.

Mary lifts another frame from the brood nest, holds it up to the sunlight, and squints at it. She is hoping to see signs of the first stage of bee development: eggs. Honey bee eggs look remarkably like grains of white rice, although they are smaller and hard to see with the naked eye.

super by super, carefully putting each component exactly where it was when she began. She records everything she has observed in her notebook and then takes a few minutes to contemplate the hive she has just visited.

At the base of the hive tower is the entrance, and bees are coming and going at an incredible rate. Field bees, the ones responsible for collecting food for the hive, arrive with clumps of bright orange-yellow pollen. Mary knows these bees are also carrying nectar, and she can't help but smile as they lumber onto the landing board in front of the hive entrance.

"They can barely negotiate the landing!" she says.

Guard bees examine the arriving bees to be sure they belong here, and receiver bees stand ready to unload the incoming nectar. When the guards are satisfied, the field bees regurgitate nectar directly into the mouths of receiver bees, who quickly store it inside the hive. New field bees constantly emerge from the hive and fly off in search of more food.

"It's like a busy airport strip," says Mary. She touches the side of the hive before moving toward the next tower in her apiary. There is little time for rest in a healthy and productive bee yard . . . not for the bees, and not for their keeper.

ABOVE: Bees enter and exit the hive from the opening at the bottom of the brood nest. The wooden platform outside the opening is called, appropriately, the landing board.

Dave (left) and Davey Hackenberg pose beside one of the eighteen-wheeled flatbed trucks they use to haul honey bees around the country. The flatbed can hold five hundred beehives at a time; the hives shown here are empty.

On November 12, 2006, Dave Hackenberg set out to inspect four hundred of his three thousand beehives. Yes, you read that right: Dave manages *three thousand* hives of honey bees. Keeping bees is Dave's full-time job, and the company he runs with his son Davey—Hackenberg Apiaries—has been producing honey and other bee products for more than forty years.

Dave left four hundred hives in an old carnival lot in Florida two months earlier, but now the owner of the lot needed the space. Dave had to inspect his hives and move them to a new location.

Inspecting and moving four hundred beehives is not a one-man job, so Dave brought along Davey and another company employee. The three men arrived at the lot late in the afternoon, wearing bee suits and carrying smokers. They also brought a forklift to help load the hives, which were stacked on wooden pallets, onto their flatbed truck. The bees had enjoyed eight weeks of warm weather and plentiful nectar, so Dave expected them to be in good shape.

They weren't.

"I told Davey to get on the forklift and I ran the smoker. I realized right off there wasn't a lot of bees flying. I started smoking a couple pallets of bees anyway, probably four or five. Then I said, *Wait a minute. There are no bees in these entrances!* So I started jerking covers off the hives. And they were empty. They were just totally empty."

Dave has been keeping bees since he was fifteen years old. In the years since then he had seen a lot of things go wrong in his beehives. He'd seen bees die of starvation over the winter and he'd seen nasty bacterial infections that can be stopped only by burning the hives. He'd seen wax moth infestations and he'd lost hives to bears and to vandals. More recently, Dave had seen the spread of small hive beetles, Varroa mites, and tracheal mites into his hives—three pests that did not even exist in the United States when he was starting out in 1962. Dave had seen a lot, but never in all his beekeeping life had he seen anything like this: Twenty million honey bees had simply vanished.

BELOW: Dave Hackenberg working his bees.

"I got frantic," he remembers. "You know, I hadn't found a beehive yet that had any bees in it. I mean, they were just completely empty. It's like someone took a sweeper and swept things clean. I got down on my hands and knees looking for dead bodies on the ground, but they just weren't there."

A closer look at the hives only added to Dave's confusion. Each contained healthy brood and enormous honey stores—a few of the hives even contained a queen. It is very unusual for adult bees to abandon their young, their food, *and* their queen. The runaway bees would not survive without these things, just as the queen would not survive without the support of the colony.

Stranger still, the abandoned hives

should have been crawling with insects stealing the unguarded honey. This sort of robbing is inevitable, but Dave found absolutely no signs of it. It was as if something was in the hives, something so awful that the bees who lived there were forced to leave, something so sinister that other insects refused to enter, even for free honey.

Dave needed to figure out what had happened to his bees, and he needed to figure it out quickly. It was too late to save these 400 hives, but he and Davey had 2,600 others to worry about.

Hackenberg Apiaries produces more than 150,000 pounds of honey per year, but their main business is renting beehives to fruit and vegetable farmers. Honey bees are efficient pollinators, and moving millions of them into a crop field while plants are blooming is a good way for farmers to ensure plentiful crops.

You see, fruit and vegetable plants reproduce by making seeds and packaging them inside an armor of edible fruit. Animals eat the fruit and then spread the seeds by discarding them or passing them when they defecate, or poop. In this way an otherwise immobile plant is

This cluster of empty beehives once housed thriving honey bee colonies. These lost hives, called deadouts, are a natural part of any beekeeping operation.

LEFT: The yellow dust on this foraging honey bee is pollen from the crocus flower she is visiting.

INSET: The basic parts of a flower. A nectar-producing organ, or nectary, is often located at the base of a flower; foraging bees rub against stamens and carpels on the way to the nectary.

able to spread itself around. It's a clever plan, really, but it works only if plants are able to make seeds in the first place. And that requires a plant to bring together its "male" parts (pollen grains) and its "female" parts (ovules). The process of transferring pollen grains to the vicinity of the ovule is called pollination, and hairy, nectar-loving honey bees are very good at it.

As the bees forage deep inside flowers in search of nectar, they rub against pollen-producing organs (stamens). Pollen grains get stuck in their body hairs and oftentimes get unstuck in just the right place: on top of a flower's ovule-producing organs (carpels). When this happens, the plant is one crucial step closer to making a seed and its surrounding fruit. Is it any wonder that farmers are anxious to have Dave's bees living in their fields while crops are in bloom?

Wind, rain, spiders, and other animals can pollinate plants, but nothing does the job as efficiently as the honey bee. Some crops, such as almonds, are so dependent on honey bees that they couldn't be produced

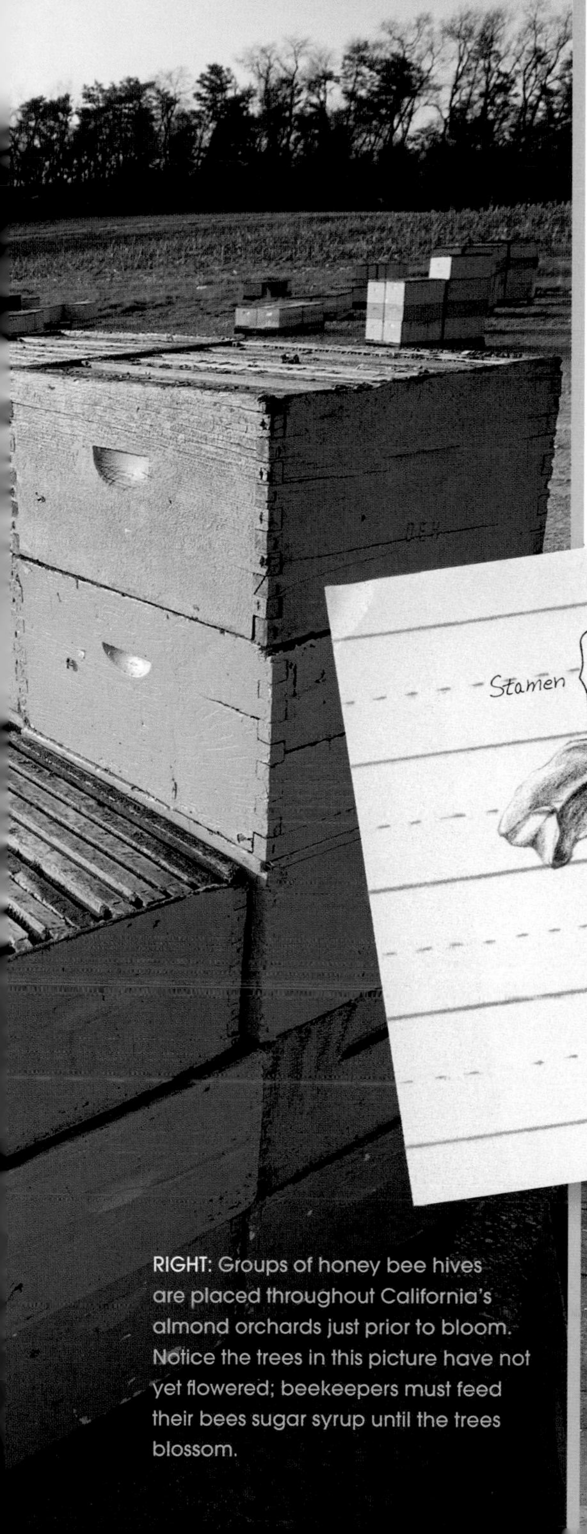

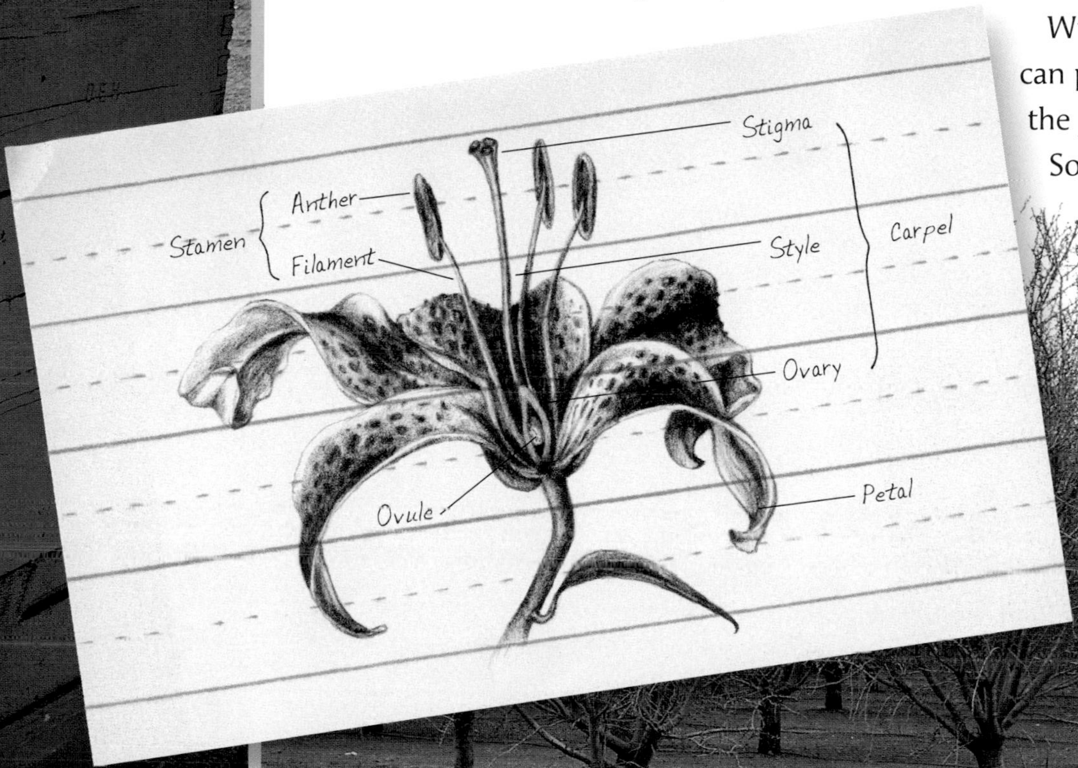

Stigma
Anther
Stamen
Filament
Style
Carpel
Ovary
Ovule
Petal

RIGHT: Groups of honey bee hives are placed throughout California's almond orchards just prior to bloom. Notice the trees in this picture have not yet flowered; beekeepers must feed their bees sugar syrup until the trees blossom.

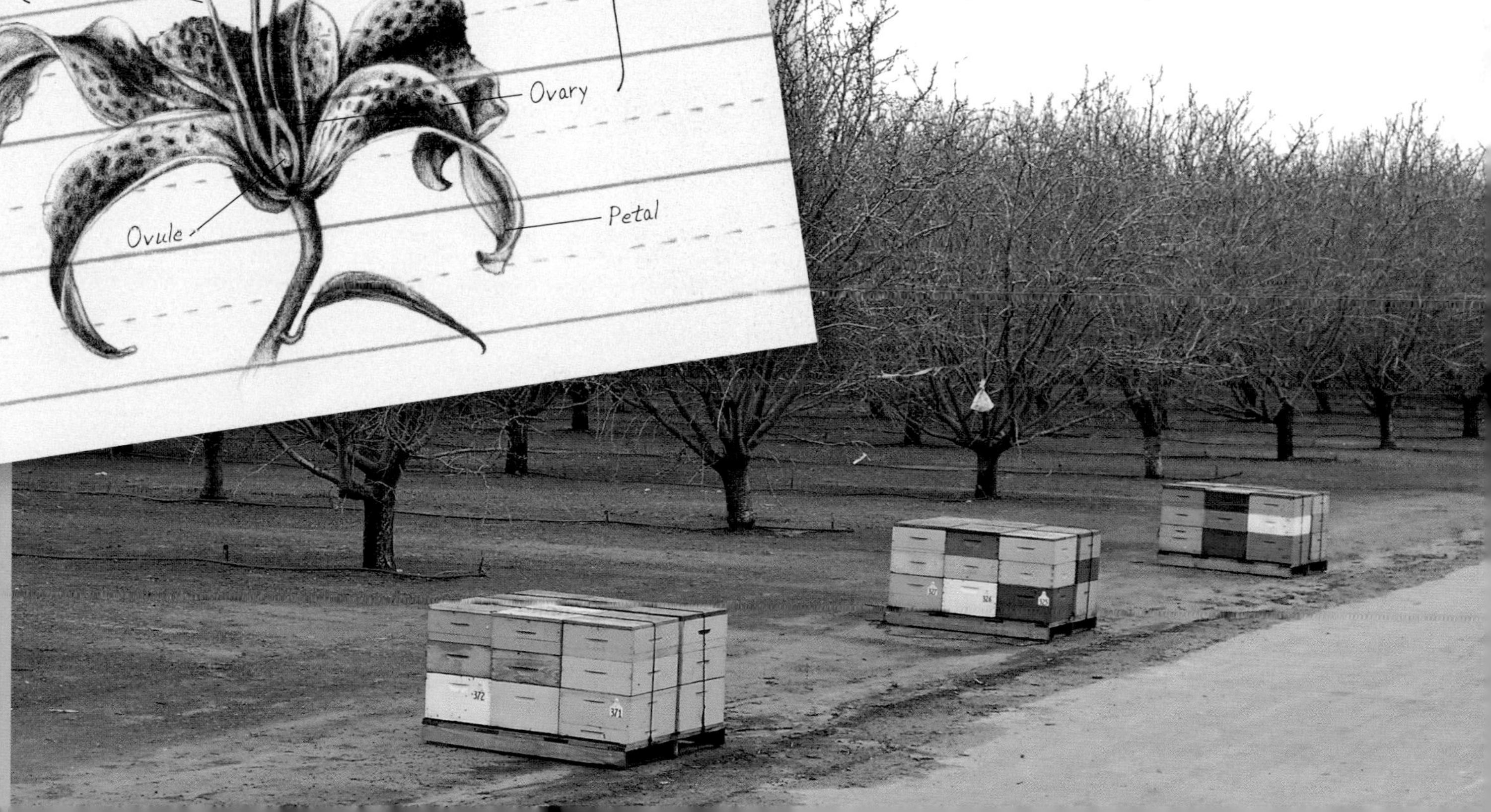

without the help of commercial bee-keepers. Every February, more than half a million acres of almond trees bloom in California, and beekeepers from around the country truck in more than one million bee colonies to do the pollinating.

Other crops depend on commercial honey bees too. In addition to California almond trees in February, Dave's bees pollinate Florida citrus trees in March, Pennsylvania apple trees in April and May, Maine blueberry bushes in June, and Pennsylvania pumpkin plants in July.

"The biggest thing about bees is not honey," says Dave. "It's that your food supply depends on them."

That means that our food supply is also dependent on the commercial beekeepers who manage bee populations year round. It is, at times, a thankless job.

RIGHT: Field bees communicate inside the hive.

BELOW: Thousands of honey bee hives wait in holding yards across California's central valley before being moved into the almond groves.

"In all my years of beekeeping," says Dave, who measures his year not in months but in fruits and vegetables, "I have only ever been home for Father's Day one time. I'm always in blueberries."

When the long and strenuous pollination season ends, the Hackenbergs bring their bees home to Pennsylvania. There, in a hilltop bee yard, they harvest and package honey. They also do other beekeeping chores, such as making splits (dividing one large colony into two smaller ones), inspecting and treating colonies for pests and diseases, and assessing the health of each colony's queen.

It is late fall when the year's work is finally finished, and there is time for one last move before winter sets in. Dave and Davey load up their three thousand hives and head to Florida. It takes six trips to move all 150 million bees south. Why do they do it? Think of it as spring training for honey bees.

Baseball teams—especially those that play ball in parts of the country where winters are long and snowy—get a jump on the new season by heading to warmer climates where they can get outside, flex their muscles, and prepare early for the season ahead. Dave Hackenberg brings

ABOVE: **Beekeepers take care of business in Dave Hackenberg's Pennsylvania apiary.**

15

his bees to Florida for the same reasons.

Instead of clustering inside the hive in a hibernation-like state, which is how bees survive frigid northern winters, Dave's bees spend the winter months maintaining their hive, rearing young, and collecting nectar and pollen. Since very few plants flower in winter, even in Florida, Dave gives his bees sugar syrup (a nectar substitute) and protein patties (a pollen substitute) to supplement their diet. This wintertime regimen of steady exercise and good food keeps the bees in shape so that when spring arrives—a time when northern bees are still dozing—Dave's team is ready to start another pollination season.

Once his bees are in Florida for the winter, Dave can usually relax. In fact, November is often his quietest month. But not in 2006, the year twenty million of his pollinators vanished without a trace.

"I'm an activist," says Dave. "I got something wrong and I call someone up to talk about it."

And so when Dave recovered from the shock of finding four hundred empty hives in a lot that had recently been home to four hundred healthy hives, he called beekeepers and bee scientists and the state bee inspectors of both Pennsylvania and Florida. He called everyone he could think of who might be able to explain what he had just seen. No one could. In fact, when news that Hackenberg Apiaries was suffering from some strange new ailment began to filter around the industry, other beekeepers wondered out loud if Dave and Davey had simply mismanaged their hives. Some even nicknamed the alleged disease Hack's Hoax.

But it wasn't long before beekeepers from across the country began to whisper about strange happenings in their own bee yards. Adult bee populations were suddenly shrinking. The hives in question contained healthy brood, a healthy queen, and plenty of food. In many cases the hive would empty completely in a very short time, and for some reason the hives stayed empty. Wax moths and hive beetles took their time moving into the abandoned hives. Eventually the whis-

A field bee working.

LEFT: A smoker smoking in an apiary.

pered rumors turned into a terrible roar: Hack's Hoax was not a hoax at all. It was the beginning of a very real and very scary honey bee catastrophe.

As more and more beekeepers came forward with stories of colony collapse, Dave continued to make phone calls and write letters. By early 2007, he had helped open discussions with scientists in France, where a similar honey bee die-off had recently occurred. Dave also gained the attention of the United States Congress, which launched an official review of the honey bee losses. Around the same time, the *New York Times* published a story called "Honeybees Vanish, Leaving Keepers in Peril," and soon papers all over the country were sounding the alarm: Our nation's honey bees were disappearing, our food supply was at risk, and no one knew what to do about it. Reporters wrote of breakfasts, lunches, and dinners without fruits and vegetables. People put forth one theory after another—genetically modified crops, cell phone signals, an act of God, and terrorist plots were each charged with the crime of wiping out honey bees.

Amid this confusion, a group of scientists joined forces with beekeepers to investigate the so-called colony collapse disorder (CCD for short).

Four of these scientists—Dennis vanEngelsdorp, Jeff Pettis, Diana Cox-Foster, and Maryann Frazier—set out to examine the most probable theories:

- an existing bee pest
- a new and deadly bee germ
- pesticides

The goal of these hive detectives was simple: figure out what was killing honey bees . . . and stop it.

BELOW: Although newspapers around the world reported otherwise, cell phones don't appear to harm honey bees.

Dennis vanEngelsdorp

Acting State Apiarist
Pennsylvania Department of Agriculture,
Harrisburg, Pennsylvania

Specialty: *Field sampling and bee autopsies*

Why bees? *I thought I'd be a horticulturist—a gardener. I even had my own gardening company. But then I took a course in beginning beekeeping and I loved it. So I bought a few hives.*

Lifetime stings: *Too many to count.*

For the record: When he is not researching bees or keeping bees or gardening with bees, Dennis can often be found making art . . . with bees.

Jeffery S. Pettis, Ph.D.

Research Leader
U.S. Department of Agriculture,
Bee Research Laboratory,
Beltsville, Maryland

Specialty: *Field sampling bees and analyzing for the presence of well-known bee pests*

Why bees? *I grew up around bees in Georgia; the neighbors had them and nearby farmers had them. Later I studied biology and entomology and eventually volunteered to help teach a bee class. I got hooked.*

Worst sting: *On the tip of the nose; it's impossible not to cry.*

For the record: In addition to studying bees in the field and in the laboratory, Jeff keeps bees in his own backyard.

Diana Cox-Foster, Ph.D.

Professor
Pennsylvania State University,
State College, Pennsylvania

Specialty: *Analyzing bee samples for bacterial and viral pathogens*

Why bees? *As a kid I fell in love with insects. I found them totally fascinating and intriguing. I think bees are exceptionally cool because of their social nature. It's very interesting biology.*

Favorite bee: *Drones. They look like little teddy bears with wings . . . and they don't sting.*

For the record: Diana recently discovered that her great-grandmother worked with bees, too. Apparently it runs in the family!

Maryann Frazier

Senior Extension Associate
Pennsylvania State University,
State College, Pennsylvania

Specialty: *Examining pesticide levels in bees, pollen, honeycomb, and brood*

Why bees? *I had a conversation with a woman who had a hive of bees that swarmed. She started to tell me about her brother collecting that swarm of bees and I just couldn't believe that anyone would do that sort of thing!*

For the record, Maryann does that sort of thing all the time now.

On becoming a bee scientist: *I took a course in beekeeping, and I just fell in love with honey bees. Now I teach that course!*

Many beekeepers are openly wondering if the industry can survive. There are serious concerns that losses are so great that there will not be enough bees to rebuild.

—CCD Working Group, December 2006

he CCD Working Group—which included Dennis, Jeff, Diana, and Maryann, as well as other honey bee scientists from around the country—launched a full-scale investigation. Because CCD was so deadly, and because beekeepers such as Dave Hackenberg were so desperate for answers that would save their businesses, CCD scientists explored several avenues of research at once. Dennis began by surveying beekeepers and sampling beehives.

Surveys were sent to beekeepers of all sizes, from commercial keepers with thousands of hives to hobbyist keepers watching over a single backyard hive. All were was asked to report total colony losses during the 2006–7 winter season, and to answer questions about how they managed their hives. Dennis hoped that their answers would turn up some clue as to what might be causing CCD.

The job of sampling beehives was a bit more complex. Dennis and his team traveled to apiaries around the country and collected live bees for further study.

LEFT: Sampled hives are numbered to help scientists track the colonies after sampling.

CCD scientists sample beehives in California.

How do you collect live bees for further study? For starters, you suit up. You also prepare a well-fueled smoker, organize your tools, and work quickly, because by the time you're finished gathering bee samples, tens of thousands of angry bees will be flying.

Sampling begins the same way an inspection does: Dennis opens a hive and removes a single frame. To gather the bees crawling over it, he slams the frame against the bottom of a shallow plastic basin. This shakedown doesn't hurt the bees, but it riles them up. With a measuring cup, Dennis scoops the shaken bees into a funnel, which, surprisingly, they pour through like liquid. He fills tubes, stores them on ice, and pours the remaining bees back into the hive. The sampled bees don't survive long on ice, but Dennis thinks of their sacrifice as the means to an important end.

"There are a lot of things killing our bees," he says, "and we need to figure out what those things are."

Since one symptom of CCD is empty beehives, there were often very few, if any, bees for Dennis to collect. He took

LEFT: Dennis prepares to gather bees in his sample basin.

RIGHT: Bees being poured through a funnel and into a plastic storage bottle.

ABOVE: Bees are stored in alcohol or on dry ice until they can be brought back to the laboratory for further study.

what bees and bee bodies he could from the collapsed hives and then sampled the next closest thing: hives that seemed to be suffering from CCD but had not yet collapsed completely. He hoped collecting bees from weak hives before they collapsed would help him discover what was causing the bees to leave.

Dennis also collected bees from healthy hives. These healthy bee samples would provide an important comparison for the CCD experiments. Anything thought to be responsible for CCD should be found in bees from the CCD hives and, by definition, *not found* in bees from the healthy hives.

Finally, because so little was known about what was causing CCD, Dennis and his team also collected pollen, wax, and brood from all the hives they sampled. Whatever was killing the bees could be in the bees themselves, but it might also be hidden in some other part of the hive.

LEFT: Dennis uses a tiny spatula to scoop stored pollen out of comb cells and into a sample tube.

ABOVE: Tubes of bee, pollen, and wax samples are bundled in plastic bags and stored in a laboratory freezer until scientists are ready to study them.

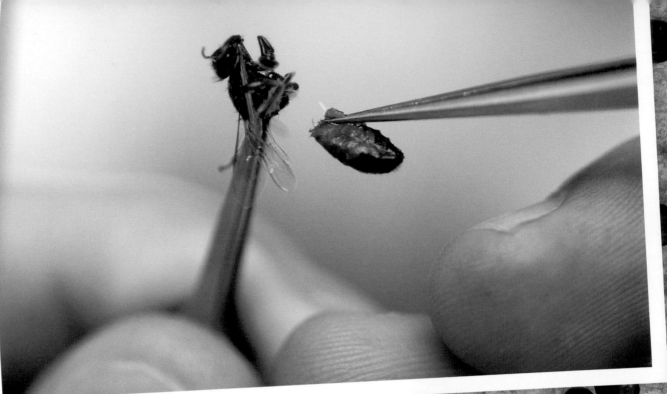

ABOVE: The abdomen is removed from a sample bee in order to prepare it for autopsy.

Dennis sent some of his samples to other scientists, stored some in freezers for future study, and set to work examining some of them himself. He and his colleagues cut sample bees open and looked inside their bodies. Using small tweezers, they pulled out gastrointestinal tracts, venom sacs, sting glands, and other organs from thousands of CCD and healthy bees. They examined these parts closely, looking for signs of disease and distress. The results of these autopsies were dramatic and conclusive: Bees from CCD hives were very, very sick.

"It was clear there was an awful lot of stuff in the CCD bees that I didn't understand, and that I couldn't find reference to anywhere," Dennis says.

Among this "stuff" were striking changes in the way the bees' internal organs looked under a microscope. Dennis found swollen, discolored, and scarred

24

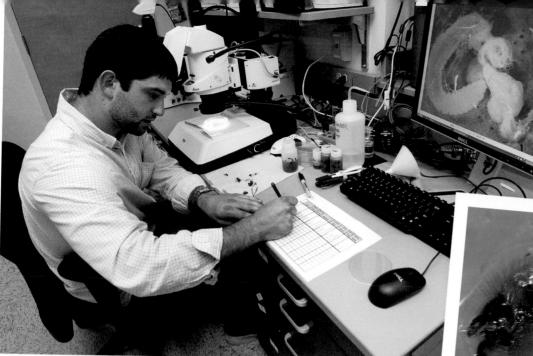

ABOVE: A scientist performing bee autopsies in the laboratory.

BELOW: Cross sections of the thorax region of two sample bees. The bee on the left is from a hive diagnosed with CCD, and the bee on the right is from a healthy hive. The inner tissues of the CCD bee are soft and discolored.

tissues and organs throughout the bodies of bees from CCD hives. The CCD bees also contained evidence of yeast, bacterial, *and* fungal infections, often all in the same bee. These abnormalities weren't seen in bees from healthy hives.

Although the autopsies didn't tell Dennis exactly what was causing colony collapse disorder, they did provide an important clue: Whatever was causing CCD was affecting the health of honey bees in a general way. Affected bees didn't have a single specific disease; they had several problems—swollen tissues, discolored organs, and multiple infections—all at the same time. *Something* was making these honey bees so sick that they could no longer fight off routine infections.

But what?

These cells contain pollen collected from different flower sources.

Honeycomb

The basic building block of a honey bee hive is the honeycomb cell. Wax for building the cells is produced by the bees themselves, in special glands on the underside of the abdomen. Using legs and mouthparts, worker bees maneuver and shape the wax flakes into hexagonal-shaped cavities, or cells. Cells are built side by side and back to back, resulting in two-sided honeycomb sheets that contain thousands of cells on each side. The sheets are hung so that there is room for bees to walk—and work—between them. Individual honeycomb cells will eventually house the hive's food stores and developing bees.

Pollen and Nectar

A healthy beehive requires enough pollen and nectar to feed its entire population in good times (when flowers are blooming) and in bad (when flowers are not blooming). Both products are collected by field bees and carried to the hive for storage. Pollen is stored in the brood nest, where it nourishes both adult and developing bees. A portion of the nectar collected by the hive's field bees is also stored in the brood nest and used as food. The majority of the nectar, however, is converted into honey and stored above the brood nest.

Honey

The process of turning nectar into honey begins inside the body of the field bee that collects it. The nectar is temporarily stored in the field bee's honey stomach, where it mixes with natural bee proteins. Even more proteins are added when the field bee transfers the nectar to the honey stomach of the receiver bee that carries it into the hive. The receiver bee transfers the nectar into a honeycomb cell and proceeds to blow bubbles through it. The bubbles help mix the nectar and the bee proteins, and also encourage the evaporation of water. When the water content of nectar reaches 18 percent it is considered ripe and will be capped by worker bees. This capped honey is very stable and will be used by the hive when times are lean . . . unless the beekeeper collects it first!

A CCD researcher weighs a sample of honey bees.

A close-up look at two Varroa mites.

Bees are critical players in our ecosystem. They enhance our way of life, whether we realize it or not. If we don't act now, colony collapse disorder will have a stinging impact on America's agricultural industry and our standard of living.

—Congressman Alcee L. Hastings (Florida), March 2007

When asked by survey what they thought was killing their hives, beekeepers responded clearly: known hive pests. Beekeepers had been dealing with three of the worst hive pests—two blood-sucking mites and a gut parasite that gives bees diarrhea—for nearly a decade. Without treatment, each can spread through a hive and eventually kill its entire population. Since beekeepers thought CCD was somehow related to these familiar creatures, Jeff Pettis set out to carefully explore the possibility.

"The main thing I've been doing in the lab is looking for Varroa, Nosema, and tracheal mites," says Jeff. "It's pretty straightforward stuff."

Straightforward? Perhaps. Disgusting? Absolutely.

Let's start with Varroa mites. These are tiny insects (about the size of this letter *o*) that survive by attaching themselves to the outside of a bee and feeding on its blood. Varroa mites spend the early part of their life cycle hidden inside a honeycomb cell, usually underneath a growing larva. When the larva is fed by adult bees, the hidden mite is fed, too. Later, when the cell is capped and the larva begins to pupate, female mites lay eggs. The eggs hatch and dozens of newborn mites attach themselves to the developing bee. In many cases the bee will die. If the bee does survive, it will emerge from its capped cell unhealthy, misshapen, and covered in a new generation of Varroa mites. These young mites hop from one bee to the next until they find a new larval cell to hide in and begin the cycle again.

ABOVE: Varroa mites attack bees the way ticks attack humans; this bee has a large mite just behind its head.

ABOVE: Sample bees are ground up in liquid.

To determine the number of Varroa mites on the bees that Dennis had collected in the field, Jeff and his colleagues used a simple shake-and-count method. Bees were placed in a large plastic bottle with liquid and shaken vigorously by machine for thirty minutes. This treatment loosened the Varroa mites attached to bees in the sample. Scientists poured the sample through a screen to trap the bee bodies; the liquid and smaller bits of debris (including mites) flowed right through. A second straining, this time through a cloth, trapped the smaller debris in a pile that researchers could easily pick through. The number of mites in each sample were counted and recorded.

If Varroa mites were playing a role in CCD, one would expect to find more of them in the samples of bees from CCD colonies. But Jeff and his team found roughly the same amount of mites in the CCD colonies and the healthy colonies. As troublesome as they are, blood-sucking Varroa mites do not appear to be involved in colony collapse disorder.

"Varroa mites are still enemy number one," warns Jeff, "and they can cause damage that persists in the hive even after you kill them."

But, he says, the mites don't appear to be the primary cause of CCD.

The next pest on Jeff's list was the tracheal mite. These mites are much smaller than Varroa, but they survive in a similar way: by finding a

ABOVE: A scientist in the bee lab searches ground-up bee samples for signs of Nosema.

safe spot—in this case a bee's breathing tubes—settling in, and then sucking the life out of a bee.

"In order to see tracheal mites you need to dissect the bees and look at their breathing tubes under a microscope," Jeff explains.

A bee's breathing tubes are located in its thorax, the middle body segment. In order to dissect them, scientists remove the head and first set of legs from the bee, then slice the thorax into thin discs. These discs are examined under a microscope for a visual identification of the tiny, egg-shaped tracheal mites.

Jeff's colleagues searched both CCD and healthy bee samples for signs of tracheal mites, but struck out a second time.

"We just didn't find tracheal mites," Jeff says. "They were almost nonexistent in CCD hives and in healthy hives."

The last bee pest that Jeff and his team looked for was a single-celled parasite called Nosema. Nosema infects the gut of bees, damaging the digestive tract and causing a form of diarrhea. Loose feces (poop) is normal for bees. In fact, their red-orange splatters are often visible on the white suits worn by beekeepers in the field. (In an apiary that is home to thousands of bees, a beekeeper is bound to get hit now and again.)

In general, however, bees are exceedingly clean. They rarely empty their bowels in the hive. Even in winter, healthy bees prefer to fly outside and away from the hive to relieve themselves. Nosema-infected bees, however, aren't able to control their bowel movements; they are forced to defecate in and around the hive, leaving a distinct red-orange splatter wherever they go.

Aside from drippy reddish markings on the outside of a hive, the only way to identify a Nosema infection is to look for the organism itself inside the bee gut. In the laboratory this is accomplished by grinding a sample of bees in a glass mortar and pestle and looking at the resulting soup under a microscope.

As with Varroa mites and tracheal mites, Jeff and his colleagues found no connection between Nosema infection and CCD.

Strike three.

Inside the Hive: Who's Who?

There are three types of adult honey bee: drones, workers, and queens. The queen is biggest. Her extra-long abdomen is full of egg-laying machinery. Drones are male bees; they are smaller than queens, with rounder abdomens and enormous eyes that meet on the top of the head. Worker bees are females; they are the smallest and most numerous bees in the hive. Of the fifty thousand bees in the average peak-of-summer honey bee hive, one is a queen, 2,000 are drones, and the remaining 47,999 are workers.

Drone

Look up the word drone in the dictionary and you'll find this definition: "an idle person who lives off others; a loafer." Male honey bees are called drones because, well, they ARE loafers. They perform no work to feed or maintain the hive and instead rely on the worker bee population to provide food, water, and shelter. They also let the workers raise the young, build and repair the honeycomb, and clean and protect the hive. In fact, the drone's one and only job is to mate with a new queen. Loafers, indeed!

Queen

The queen bee is as busy as her workers, but not with housekeeping, child rearing, or food production. The queen's job is to lay eggs . . . lots of them. As soon as she is able, a young queen embarks on the first of her mating flights. She mates with several drones, storing the sperm she collects in a special organ in her abdomen. From the moment she returns to the hive until the moment she dies, typically a span of one to three years, the queen bee lays eggs. At the height of her powers, she can lay two thousand eggs a day, seven days a week.

Keepers often mark their queens with a spot of paint.

Worker

Workers, on the other hand, are the muscle of the honey bee colony. During her six-week lifespan, a worker bee develops the ability to perform almost every job in the hive. The youngest workers are housekeepers and nurse bees. As her wax-producing glands develop, a worker takes on the building and repairing of honeycomb. Soon she is able to make honey, guard the hive, and experiment with flights outside. The oldest workers are field bees, who spend their days collecting nectar, pollen, propolis, and water for the colony. Field bees have the most dangerous of all worker jobs; most don't survive long.

Overall, U.S. beekeepers suffered an average loss of 38% of their colonies during the winter of 2006–2007 . . . between 651,000 and 875,000 of the nation's estimated 2.4 million colonies were lost.

—*American Bee Journal,* July 2007

Diana Cox-Foster is an expert on honey bee viruses. While Dennis was performing bee autopsies and Jeff was looking for signs of known honey bee pests, Diana was working to determine which of the known honey bee viruses could be found in CCD bees. Her initial studies verified what researchers already knew: CCD bees were very sick.

"We found that the remaining bees in collapsing colonies were harboring every known virus that we could detect using our methods," Diana says. "Having this huge number of viruses in each of these individual bees from the colony is quite unusual."

Viruses are constantly present in the environment. For example, virus particles—like those that cause the flu in humans—are released into the air

whenever an infected person coughs or sneezes. These particles can infect a healthy person when he or she breathes in the infected air. This is one way that humans "catch" the flu. Although bees don't cough or sneeze, they do spread virus particles. The spreading happens mainly at feeding sites, where infected bees leave virus-loaded spit on the flowers they visit. The next bee to visit that flower has a good chance of picking up the virus, bringing it back to her hive, and spreading it even further.

"Viral particles end up in the hive's food supply," Diana explains, "and from there are transmitted throughout the entire colony."

Based on the rapid spread of colony collapse disorder and on the variety of infections found in CCD bees, Diana began to suspect a fast-spreading and powerful virus had infected the bees,

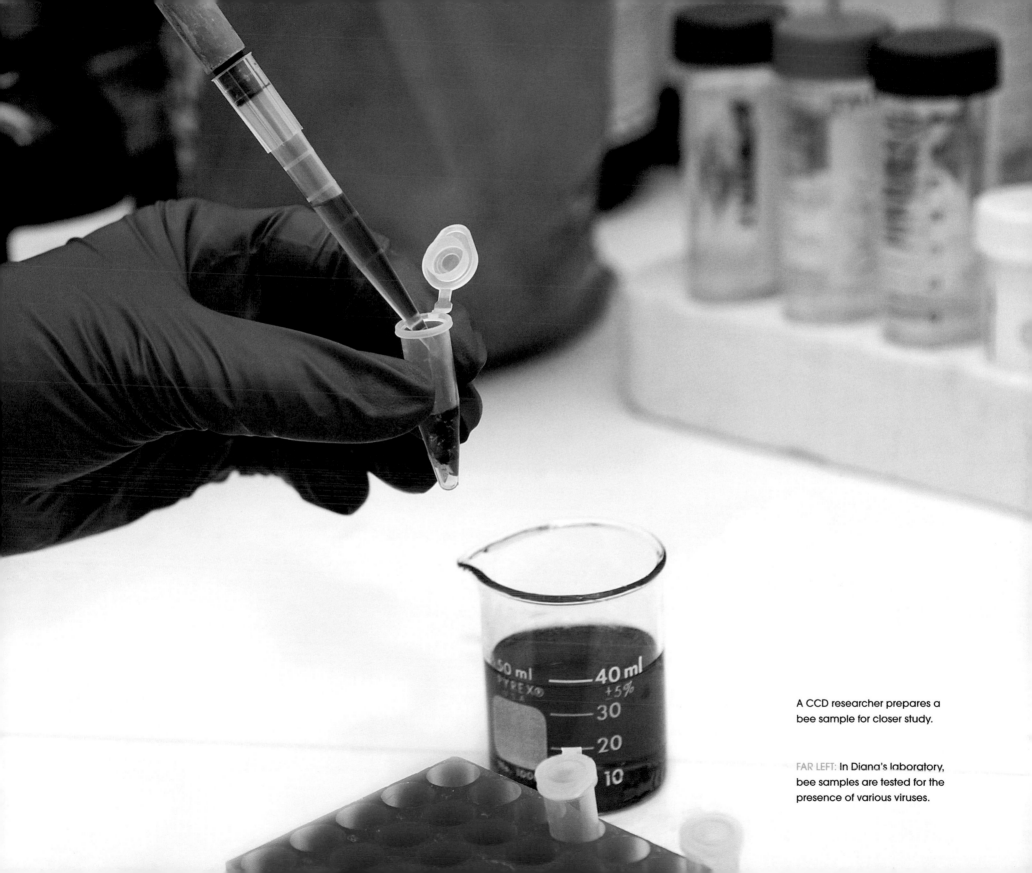

A CCD researcher prepares a bee sample for closer study.

FAR LEFT: In Diana's laboratory, bee samples are tested for the presence of various viruses.

perhaps a virus that had not yet been identified by honey bee scientists. The new virus, if it existed, might be powerful enough to weaken the infected bees such that they were unable fight off other infections.

To test her theory, Diana recruited a group of scientists who hunt for human viruses to help her comb honey bee samples for as-yet-undiscovered bee viruses. And though they did not find a new virus, they did discover that one of the known honey bee viruses was present in almost all the CCD samples. Interestingly, this virus was absent from almost every healthy sample.

"We analyzed more than twelve hundred bees," says Diana, "and found something called the Israeli acute paralysis virus (IAPV) in CCD bees."

Showing that the new virus correlated with colony collapse disorder—that is, that colonies in which the virus was detected usually had CCD and colonies in which the virus was not present rarely had CCD—was a major breakthrough. Finally scientists had a concrete way of diagnosing CCD hives. But Diana's results did not prove that the new virus caused CCD. To do that, Diana would have to expose a healthy hive to the virus and show that the bees in it developed the disorder.

Unfortunately, injecting a live virus into a healthy colony of bees is a very dangerous thing to do. Remember that bees live outside and are, for the most part, free to roam anywhere. There was no way for Diana to ensure that bees from her newly infected hive didn't

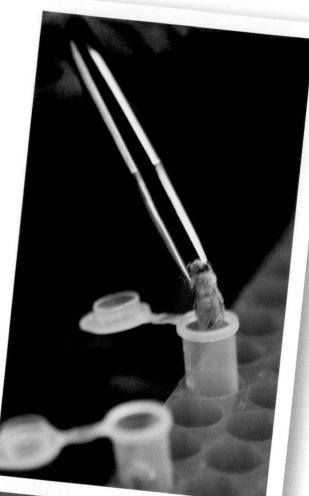

ABOVE: Scientists in Diana's lab are able to identify virus particles from a single bee.

LEFT: This greenhouse on the campus of Pennsylvania State University is the site of Diana's indoor honey bee experiments.

carry the virus out into the field, leave it on flowers, and thus pass it along to healthy colonies. This sort of experiment, if conducted, might make the CCD problem even worse than it already was.

So Diana got creative. She decided to try the experiment indoors, where the bees she infected with virus could be contained. Indoors, her bees would not come into contact with other bees and therefore could not spread the virus or disease in the wild.

Hold on. Can honey bees be raised *indoors?*

Well, not yet. But Diana and her team are close to setting up a functioning indoor bee yard. They have been raising bees in a multiroom, airtight greenhouse. In place of nectar from wild-

flowers, the bees forage sugar syrup from a hanging feeder. In place of pollen, they eat protein patties specially formulated to keep them healthy. If Diana can establish conditions that let the bees survive indoors, she will be able to introduce IAPV into bees in one room of the greenhouse and compare the fate of those bees to uninfected bees being raised in the greenhouse room next door.

There are other advantages to greenhouse experiments, too.

RIGHT: Just like her foraging sisters outdoors, this greenhouse honey bee gets covered with pollen while feeding.

"Part of the problem now," Diana says of the past CCD studies, "is that most of the bees from a collapsing colony are never found. In a greenhouse we should be able to find the dead bees."

Diana's results were published in the journal *Science* and discussed in newspapers and magazines around the world. But she and the other hive detectives remain cautious about their discovery.

"IAPV is a leading candidate at this point in time," she says. "But we don't think it can work by itself to cause CCD in bees."

The main reason Diana doesn't believe the virus can work alone to cause CCD is that she and others have found the virus in honey bee samples dating back to 2002, four years before the CCD catastrophe began. If this virus is involved in CCD, why didn't it cause colony collapse in 2002?

One intriguing explanation is that IAPV is just one of a series of events that have pushed honey bees into decline. Diana and the other hive detectives have begun to wonder if something in the honey bee environment has changed recently, something that could make honey bees suddenly more susceptible to the IAPV virus.

ABOVE: Dead bees litter the concrete floor of the greenhouse each day. Collecting these bees gives scientists a chance to look closely at bees that die outside the hive, something that is nearly impossible to do in outdoor apiaries.

As it turns out, a whole lot of things have changed in the honey bee environment in the past decade. First of all, the virus itself has changed: Diana's studies have shown that IAPV is a virus that evolves quickly over time. Could the current form of the virus be deadlier than earlier forms?

Honey bee nutrition has also changed in recent years, and not for the better. As

farms get larger and more specialized, the honey bees living and working on them during the pollination season are forced to survive on a single nectar and pollen source for weeks on end. Imagine eating hamburgers—*only* hamburgers—for breakfast, lunch, and dinner for six weeks straight. This is what pollinating California's almond trees might feel like for honey bees: almond pollen and almond nectar at every meal for weeks and weeks. Could this poor diet be making bees more prone to infections?

Finally, the chemicals used on farms—and inside beehives—have also changed in the past ten years. Farmers use pesticides to protect their crops and herbicides to keep down weeds. Household gardeners often use similar chemicals on their lawns and gardens. Even

beekeepers use chemicals; there are several designed to kill Varroa mites and tracheal mites. Could exposure to this long list of chemicals be weakening the bees?

As if all this wasn't bad enough, in 2007 the National Academy of Sciences released the results of a two-year study that showed pollinator species throughout North America—not just honey bees but also moths, butterflies, beetles, and other creatures—are in a serious decline.

As Diana says, "The million-dollar question becomes, Is CCD just a honey bee problem? Or is it part of a greater issue?"

LEFT: This close-up view of a frame from a greenhouse hive shows a worker bee, stored pollen, stored nectar, and eggs, indicating the hive unit is functioning indoors.

RIGHT: Bees in the greenhouse experiments are able to make honey from the sugar syrup they are given to eat, as evidenced by this frame. Because Diana's virus experiments are conducted with completely new equipment, the wax in the hives is very white in appearance.

Like all insects, honey bees have three major body segments (head, thorax, and abdomen) and six legs. They've got other interesting parts, too . . .

Proboscis

The proboscis (pro-BOSS-kiss) is part of the honey bee's mouth. Bees use the long, thin appendage for collecting water, nectar, or honey. Bees can also use the proboscis to pierce the outer petals of a flower, as in this picture, in order to access the nectar supply.

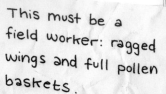

This must be a field worker: ragged wings and full pollen baskets.

Wings

Honey bees sport two sets of wings. They're for flying, of course, but wings also provide a handy way for beekeepers to estimate the age of a bee. Pristine, smooth-edged wings are the hallmark of a young honey bee, while worn and ragged wings are the badge of a worker bee that has spent days—maybe even weeks—flying outside the hive in search of supplies.

The globs of pollen in this bee's baskets are as big as her head!

Pollen Baskets

Honey bees have three pairs of segmented and hairy legs. In addition to walking, each set of legs has a unique function: the front legs are used to clean the bee's antennae; the middle legs have a spear-like hair that helps the bees to manipulate wax; and the hind legs are equipped with stiff hairs that form a basket for carrying pollen or propolis. When fully loaded, pollen baskets can carry nearly one half the weight of the bee.

Stinger

The stinger is a modified ovipositor, or egg-laying organ, which explains why it's found only in females. (That's right—drones can't sting.) Although workers can sting fellow bees with no ill effects, their barbed stingers get "stuck" in human skin. The worker bee will try with all her might to pull it loose, but the result will be disastrous. As she pulls, the stinger and other interior organs are ripped from her body. She dies soon after.

Maryann and a colleague examine a frame from their study hives.

> *Whatever it is, it's still out there and it's still killing our bees.*
>
> —Kim Flottum, CCD Editorial, *Bee Culture,* June 2008

One year after his discovery of CCD, Dave Hackenberg and his son Davey had built their beekeeping operation back up . . . and their bees looked pretty good. Father and son had devised a high protein bee feed they hoped would help their colonies deal better with the stress of, well, being a bee.

"We're pounding these bees so hard," Dave admits. "This year we're trying a lot of different things . . . We're trying to give the bees a rest."

In addition to better feed and more rest, Dave is working with the growers who rent his bees to ensure that the pesticides they treat their crops with aren't hurting his bees.

Using pesticides is a tricky business. Farmers and gardeners rely on them to protect crops from aphids, Japanese beetles, and other plant-and-fruit-chomping insects. But honey bees, which are needed to efficiently pollinate those same crops, are insects too. And it is extremely difficult to find chemicals that kill the harmful insects and leave the beneficial ones alone.

Farmers stack the deck in their favor by using pesticides that are proven safe for honey bees. They are careful to spray crops at times when honey bees are least likely to be nearby, for example, before plants bloom. But Dave and his commercial beekeeping colleagues remain concerned. Recently, Dave learned of a new class of pesticide that has become a favorite with his growers. The new pesticides, called neonicotinoids (neo-NIK-a-tin-oids), are systemic. That is, the pesticide is able to infiltrate every system of a plant.

ABOVE: **Honey bees bridging the space between frames in their hive.**

43

After a single treatment, the chemical will be found in the roots, stems, leaves, flowers, and pollen of a plant. This is great for farmers because it means a single treatment is long-lasting and deadly to a variety of crop pests. But it is not clear what this sort of systemic presence means for honey bees. If the pesticide is in the pollen, are the bees bringing it into the hive? What effect does constant exposure to these pesticides have on field bees? Or on the young bees who spend all of their time in the hive?

"Our bee losses almost parallel this whole pesticide revolution," says Dave, who is convinced

that systemic pesticides are playing a role in CCD.

Maryann Frazier, who recently began identifying chemicals found inside beehives, tends to agree with him.

"We expected that if pesticides were going to be the CCD problem, the systemics were going to be involved," she says.

In the beginning, Maryann examined pollen samples that Dennis had collected from CCD and healthy hives out in the field. With the help of several chemists, she was able to screen these pollen samples for more than 150 chemicals known to be part of the honey bee environment. These included systemic pesticides, other pesticides used by farmers, and the chemicals beekeepers use to treat mite infestations in their hives.

The first surprise was how common chemicals were; Maryann found them in almost every sample she tested, whether it came from a CCD hive or a healthy hive. Of 208 pollen samples, only three were completely chemical-free.

"It was shocking to us to find, on average, five pesticides in each pollen sample," says Maryann. "In one sample we found *seventeen* different pesticides."

ABOVE: Maryann's colleague uses an instrument designed to identify chemicals from samples. (For the record, the instrument is called a liquid chromatograph tandem mass spectrometer!)

Perhaps even more shocking was that the chemicals found most frequently—and at the highest levels—were those that beekeepers themselves put in the hive to protect their bees from Varroa mites. Somehow these beekeeper-applied chemicals were finding their way into the pollen the bees stored in the hive.

45

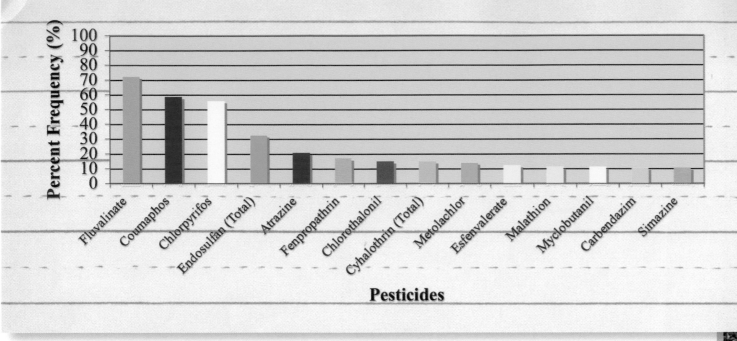

ABOVE: **This bar graph shows the percentage of pollen samples that contained the named chemicals. The two most common, Fluvalinate and Coumaphos, are pesticides that beekeepers put inside beehives in order to protect bees from Varroa mites.**

Maryann went on to test wax samples, and the results were similar. Beekeeper-applied chemicals were found in every one of the eighty-eight wax samples she tested.

Interestingly, Maryann found absolutely no correlation between chemical contamination and CCD. Pollen and wax samples from healthy beehives were just as contaminated as pollen and wax samples from CCD hives. These results put an end—once and for all—to the idea that CCD is caused by a single pest, pathogen, or chemical.

"I don't think CCD is caused by one thing. I do think it's a combination of things that are just over the top," Maryann explains. "It's like a cup that fills up. Maybe pesticides fill it halfway and viruses fill it halfway and suddenly it's overflowing. Or maybe poor nutrition is twenty-five percent and the mites and the pesticides fill up the rest. In other words, the cup fills up in different ways. But when you get to that full point, the bees just fall apart. They collapse."

Maryann will continue to examine the role of environmental chemicals in honey

Maryann collects brood samples in the field.

bee health, just as Diana will continue to examine the role of IAPV and other viruses in honey bee health and Jeff will continue to examine the role of mites and other pests. But the entire team of hive detectives is now designing experiments that allow them to examine these stresses in combination. Perhaps they will identify the combination that results in colony collapse disorder. Even if they don't, Jeff Pettis is confident that this is the right approach.

"There are a lot of different parts to this puzzle," he explains, "and we need to take a look at how these pieces come together to cause our bee problems."

Jeff spoke to an assembly of concerned beekeepers in January of 2008, and he told them to focus on the only good news to come from the CCD disaster so far: publicity.

"Think about this. If you asked the general public, 'What four things do you need to grow an apple for your table?' I'd bet they could only come up with three of them: sunlight, water, nutrients. I'd bet you money that the vast majority of the public, prior to CCD, would not have been able to name the fourth: pollinators. But now they can. Now the public knows about bees."

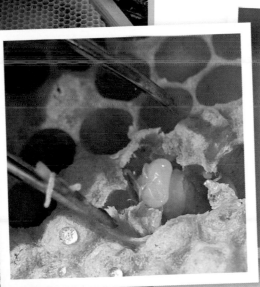

47

All three of these jars contain honey. The honey on the left was made from the nectar of knotweed flowers, the honey in the middle was made with nectar from wildflowers and goldenrod, and the honey on the right was made from the nectar of black locust trees. Thanks to the variety of sources, each honey has a unique texture, scent, and flavor.

And now for something sweet . . .

It's the middle of June—eighteen months after Dave's gruesome discovery in that Florida carnival lot—and sun shines brightly through Mary Duane's kitchen window. A dehumidifier hums in the corner, and nearly every surface in the room is covered in clear plastic.

"Someday I'll have a honey house," Mary says with a laugh, "but for now, I have the kitchen."

To prepare for our visit, Mary has also set up a screened tent in the side yard. Later in the afternoon, when she is elbow-deep in honey, she'll move some of her harvesting equipment outdoors in order for us to capture better photographs of her honey harvest.

This harvest actually began yesterday, when Mary opened each of her backyard hives and searched the honey supers for frames that were full or nearly full of capped honey. Whenever she found

one, Mary shook it sharply over the hive, which forced most of the bees to drop back in. Then she swept away the stragglers with a soft-bristled brush and stored the bee-free, honey-full frame in a covered plastic bin.

"There are other ways to remove bees from honey frames," Mary explains. "I have time, though, so I do it my way."

The twenty-four frames of honey she collected are now hanging in three hive boxes stacked one atop the other and

RIGHT: Mary typically harvests honey twice each year . . . in her kitchen. The supers on the floor are filled with honey frames (no bees!), and her extracting tools are laid out around the room.

LEFT: Decapping involves gently slicing the wax caps away from the honey frame.

set on a metal pan in the center of her kitchen floor. She estimates she'll collect nearly seventy-five pounds of honey from them today.

To get at the honey, Mary first has to cut away the wax caps. Although bee-keeping supply stores sell special knives for uncapping honey frames, Mary pre-fers a simple kitchen carving knife. Lean-ing a single frame upright on the edge of a large plastic bin, she works from the top down and uses the sharp edge of her knife to gently slice away the wax caps.

"The trick is to try not to cut too deeply," she says. "The bees will have to rebuild the parts of the comb that I cut away. I'm trying to save them some work by taking just the very, very top."

Mary lets the cut wax drop onto the grate at the bottom of the plastic bin, flips the frame, and uncaps the other side. In less than fifteen minutes she has shaved the wax surface from both sides of four honey frames and they are ready for the extractor.

ABOVE: In the safety of Mary's outdoor tent, honey frames await extraction. The frames at the back of the bin are still capped, but those on the side have had the wax layer removed. Surprisingly, very little honey drips out of the decapped frames.

OPPOSITE: This is the view looking into the extractor. The basket inside will hold two honey frames, one on either side of the center bar.

Mary's extractor is a large metal cylinder with a square wire basket inside. The basket is big enough to hold two frames of honey at once and can be attached to a hand crank on the extractor cover.

"The extractor works on the same principle as a salad spinner," Mary says as she loads the frames. "All I've got to do is load it and crank this handle."

As she cranks, the wire basket spins. Just as the rotation of a salad spinner forces water off lettuce leaves, rotation of the extractor basket forces honey out of the uncapped comb cells. The honey splashes against the walls of the extractor and slowly drips to its bottom. Mary turns the crank just long enough to force honey from the outside face of the frames. (Remember that honeycomb is two-sided.) After a minute or two she stops the extractor and flips the frames so that the inside face, which is still full of honey, can be spun dry, too.

After several more minutes of cranking, Mary removes the empty frames and inserts two full ones. When these are emptied she sets a tall white bucket—the settling bucket—under a spout at the base of the extractor. A flick of her wrist lifts the gate, and thick, golden honey pours out.

"The smell is *not* a problem," Mary says, breathing the sweet air deeply.

RIGHT: Mary's raw honey is strained into the settling bucket.

BELOW: Some people prefer their honey directly from the hive: no extraction, no waiting.

The top of the settling bucket is fitted with a strainer, and soon it is filled with honey. Although the color is familiar, this honey doesn't look like what you would buy in a grocery store. Instead, its surface is very bubbly, almost frothy, and there are lots of things floating in and on the liquid.

"Raw honey is unfiltered," explains Mary, "and there are people who absolutely love it."

And what's not to love about honey that comes with floating pollen, wax bits, and the occasional bee leg? Raw honey lovers may adore these earthy extras, but most people prefer their honey free of bee parts. The strainer Mary is using will trap the wax, bee bits, and bubbles alike. By the end of the day the bottom of the settling bucket will be filled with crystal clear blue-ribbon honey. (Mary's honey has won awards at several local fairs.)

52

ABOVE: Mary sets up her honey extracting equipment in a screened tent.

BELOW: Mary bottles her honey in a variety of jars.

ABOVE: Mary fills a glass honey jar with honey from the settling bucket.

Mary repeats the uncapping, extracting, and filtering process for all twenty-four frames of honey. Partway through the afternoon she moves the extractor to a picnic table in the outdoor tent. It's still sunny outside, and very hot. Although the heat is uncomfortable for the *harvester,* it is great for the *harvesting:* Honey flows faster when it is warm.

Within minutes of our arrival, bees are buzzing around the outside of the tent, attracted by the smell of honey. Several land on the mesh roof, making big bee shadows as they search for a way in.

"The honey is messy and sticky and I could live without it," Mary says. She gazes at the bees outside, her bees, and continues to crank the extractor. "I would keep bees anyway, even if I didn't collect the honey."

When enough filtered honey has collected in the settling bucket, Mary grabs a glass jar and sets it under the spout at the base of the bucket. This time when she opens the gate, the honey that pours out is clear.

53

While Mary cleans up the tent and the kitchen, her bees clean up the leftover wax caps. This wax/honey mix, called comb honey by beekeepers, is yummy for humans, too.

"Gold," Mary calls it. "Liquid gold."

Properly sealed in its glass container, Mary's liquid gold will stay fresh for years, possibly even decades. Occasionally the sugars in honey will crystallize, forming solids in the bottom of the jar, but crystallized honey is perfectly edible and just as delicious as liquid honey. You can scoop the crystals out and eat them or, if you prefer, heat the honey gently to dissolve them.

The color and flavor of honey depends on the source of nectar used to make it. Today's harvest is made mostly of nectar from the wildflowers and black locust trees that thrive in Mary's neighborhood. Bottled up, it is amber in color and clear enough to read the pages of this book through.

Cleaning up after a honey harvest is as hard—or maybe harder—than the extraction itself. Mary lets the bees help her whenever possible. Excess honey on the discarded wax caps, on the emptied honey frames, and on any utensils is given back to the bees. Mary simply sets the honey-covered objects outside and within minutes the bees arrive to suck them dry.

The cleaned wax caps will eventually be melted and poured into empty juice cartons for storage. When Mary is ready, she'll melt the wax again and use it to make beeswax candles, skin creams, and soaps.

The cleaned frames are put right back into the beehives. The bees will repair the damaged wax combs and eventually begin refilling the comb cells with nectar. If all goes well Mary will harvest more honey in the fall.

In spite of CCD, Mary's bees are healthy and productive. But because of what she has learned about honey bee health during the CCD crisis, Mary is more vigilant than ever about the health and safety of her bees. She works hard to protect them from pesticide exposure, uses organic mite treatments in place of harsher chemicals, encourages weed and wildflower growth in her yard so that the bees enjoy a balanced and nutritious diet, and keeps careful watch for mites, beetles, and other hive pests or diseases. She has become acutely aware of her role in both her backyard apiary and in the world: to protect honey bees. Our world is a dangerous place for them, and it will take a Herculean effort on the part of all humans—people who keep bees, people who study bees, and even people who read about bees—to see them through.

It would be impossible to fit in these eighty pages all the amazing things I have learned about honey bees while researching this book. But it would be equally impossible not to at least mention some of them. And so I have created this appendix. I hope you find something here that fascinates you...and that you'll research and write about it yourself. Enjoy!

Worker bees watch a hive-mate waggle dance.

Honey bees communicate by dancing. That's right, dancing. In order to recruit workers to a particularly good food source, returning field bees will perform a series of specific movements—the round dance or the waggle dance—within the hive. Their movements tell nearby bees how to find the foraging site.

There are more than four thousand species of bees in North America and close to twenty thousand species worldwide. Next time you are in a park or garden, sit and watch the flowers in bloom. You will be surprised by how many different bees—and bee look-alikes—show up.

Honey bees are also incredible odor detectors. Their sense of smell is so finely tuned, in fact, that scientists are able to train them to sniff out bombs, dead bodies, and other distinct odors.

Queen cells are specialized honeycomb cells built to house developing queens. A colony preparing to swarm will build several of them, and the existing queen will lay a single egg in each. When the first new queen emerges, she stakes her claim as the hive's sole monarch by marking the remaining queen cells—and the developing queens inside—for destruction by the colony.

Beekeepers are often classified by the number of hives they manage: hobbyist beekeepers (backyarders) generally keep fewer than a hundred hives, commercial beekeepers (full-timers) typically keep more than a thousand hives, and sideline beekeepers (part-timers) fall somewhere in between. All beekeepers—whether hobbyist, sideliner, or commercial—are amateur meteorologists, botanists, entomologists, and pharmacologists.

Queen cells are Peanut shaped.

Just before the new queen emerges from her special cell, the old queen leaves the colony, taking half its inhabitants with her. The swarm will settle nearby and send scouts to find a suitable site for building a new hive.

In 1956, a handful of bees that had been imported to Brazil from Africa were accidentally released into the wild. These bees went on to found an entire race of bee—the so-called Africanized bee—and became known for their highly defensive behavior. You probably know these bees by their ominous nickname: killer bees. The bee on the left (below) is an Africanized honey bee.

The oversize brood cells in this image house drones.

In a reproductive process that is unique to a small number of insects, drones develop from unfertilized eggs. That is, although the drone has a mother (either the queen or, under certain conditions, a laying worker bee), it has no father. This process is known as parthenogenesis (PAR-tha-no-JEN-i-sis).

Scientists believe that North American pollinators are in decline. American commercial farms, on the other hand, are more massive than ever. As a result, there simply aren't enough wild bees to do the pollination work necessary to grow our food. (That's why beekeepers like Dave migrate across the country.) All of us can support wild honey bees and other wild pollinator species by providing healthy habitat: lots of native flowers and no pesticides.

Our understanding of wild pollinator populations is minimal. As a result, scientists have renewed efforts to monitor wild bee populations . . . and they need your help. Check out the Bee-spotter Project (beespotter.mste.uiuc.edu), the Great Sunflower Project (www.greatsunflower.org), and the Feral Hive Project (www.savethehives.com) to learn more.

Glossary

ABDOMEN: The rearmost part of the three-segmented bee body, which houses the bee's heart, reproductive organs, digestive organs, and sting gland.

ALARM PHEROMONE: A scented chemical released by honey bees in response to stress, especially when stinging an enemy.

ANTHER: Specialized part of a flower's stamen in which pollen grains are formed.

APIARIST: A beekeeper.

APIARY: An area in which managed honey bee colonies are kept; also called a bee yard.

ATTENDANT BEE: Worker bee whose job is to feed and clean the queen bee.

BEE INSPECTOR: Beekeeper employed by the government for the purpose of inspecting hives and assisting beekeepers; most states employ a state bee inspector.

BELLOWS: Hand-operated pump for creating air currents; the bellows of a smoker allows beekeepers to blow smoke into the hives.

BROOD: Developing bees, including eggs, larvae, and pupae.

BROOD NEST: Part of the hive where brood is raised.

BURR COMB: Honeycomb built in parts of the hive not intended for this use.

CAP: Refers to the wax that bees lay on top of ripened honey and developing brood; also called capping.

CARPEL: The female reproductive organ of a flower.

CCD: Colony collapse disorder, the name used to describe a huge and as-yet-unexplained die-off of managed honey bee colonies around the world.

COLONY: Family of honey bees living together in a hive, including workers, drones, and a single queen.

COMMERCIAL BEEKEEPER: Full-time beekeeper who manages thousands of beehives, usually for both honey production and pollination services.

DEADOUT: Used to describe a hive in which a colony of bees has died.

DRONE: Male honey bee.

FORAGE: To search for food; the location where such food is found can be called a foraging site.

FOUNDATION: Thin sheet of wax provided by the beekeeper in a wooden frame and on which the bees build their honeycomb.

FRAME: A wooden support, rectangular in shape, which holds two-sided sheets of honeycomb in a managed beehive.

GUARD BEE: Worker bee that monitors the hive entrance.

HERBICIDE: A substance that kills plants.

HIVE TOOL: Metal gadget used by bee-keepers to pry apart the components of a managed beehive.

HOBBY BEEKEEPER OR HOBBYIST: Beekeeper who manages one or more hives of bees, usually for the purpose of collecting honey.

HONEY: Flower nectar that has been gathered by bees, stored in honeycomb, and concentrated by evaporation.

LARVA: The grublike stage of honey bee development; the larva hatches from an egg and eventually transforms into a pupa (plural is *larvae*).

MIGRATORY BEEKEEPERS: Beekeepers who move their apiary sites; many commercial beekeepers are migratory, trucking their hives between pollination sites across the country.

MITE: Tiny insect parasite whose life cycle is intertwined with that of honey bees.

MITICIDE: A chemical that kills mites.

NECTAR: Sugary substance produced by most flowers and collected by honey bees in order to produce honey.

NECTARY: Part of a flowering plant that secretes nectar.

NURSE BEE: Worker bee whose role in the hive involves feeding and caring for developing bees in the brood nest.

OVIPOSITOR: An egg-laying organ.

OVULE: Plant structure that contains female reproductive material.

PARTHENOGENESIS: Reproductive process in which females produce off-spring from unfertilized eggs.

PATHOGEN: A disease-producing organism.

POLLEN: The male reproductive material of plants; pollen is used by bees and many other insects as a source of proteins and nutrition.

POLLEN BASKETS: A device on the hind leg of worker bees made of specialized hairs and used to store and transport pollen from the field to the hive.

POLLINATION: The transfer of pollen grains from the anther (part of the stamen) to the stigma (part of the carpel) within or between flowers.

POLLINATOR: An animal that can carry out the transfer of pollen grains from the anther to the stigma of a flower.

PROBOSCIS: Mouthpart of a honey bee; used to gather nectar and water.

PROPOLIS: Sticky substance produced by plants and trees and collected by honey bees for use as a hive sealant.

PROTEIN: Essential multiunit molecules produced by all life forms; many proteins have specific functions.

QUEEN BEE: The only fully developed female bee in a hive; the queen bee is mother to all the bees in a hive.

RECEIVER BEE: Worker bee whose job is to collect nectar from incoming field bees.

ROBBING: The removal of honey from a weak or abandoned beehive, most often by other bees or insects.

SIDELINE BEEKEEPER: Beekeeper who manages more than one hundred but fewer than one thousand beehives; also referred to as a part-time bee-keeper.

SMOKER: A covered canister fitted with a bellows and used by beekeepers to blow smoke into beehives.

SPLITS: Smaller colonies made by dividing one large colony into two.

STAMEN: Male reproductive organ of a flower.

STIGMA: Specialized portion of a flower's female reproductive organ, or carpel; the stigma's sticky surface receives pollen.

STING GLAND: Venom-producing organ of the honey bee; venom produced in the sting gland is delivered to victims via an adapted ovipositor.

SUPER: Another name for the hive box, a four-sided open box in which frames are hung in managed beehives.

SWARM: A large group of bees—including an old queen, several drones, and thousands of workers—that leaves an overcrowded hive in search of a suitable site for establishing a new nest.

VEIL: Protective headgear worn by bee-keepers.

VIRUS: Microscopic infectious agent that reproduces in living cells; viruses often cause disease in the host organism.

WORKER BEES: Female bees with undeveloped reproductive organs; workers are responsible for all the major hive chores (except egg-laying, which is the job of the queen bee).

MATERIALS TO STUDY

Newbees (beginner beekeepers) and wannabees (folks who wish they were beginner beekeepers) will find loads of useful information in these books, magazines, and films.

BOOKS

The Life and Times of the Honeybee
By Charles Micucci
Ticknor & Fields, 1995
This illustrated book for younger readers is a great introduction to honey bees and beekeeping.

Clan Apis
By Jay Hosler, Ph.D.
Active Synapse, 2000
This is a highly readable and scientifically accurate graphic-novel introduction to honey bees and their world.

The Backyard Beekeeper
By Kim Flottum
Quarry Books, 2005
This gem is a heavily illustrated and user-friendly introduction to all aspects of keeping bees.

MAGAZINES

Bee Culture
The A.I. Root Company
623 West Liberty Street
Medina, Ohio 44256

American Bee Journal
51 South 2nd Street
Hamilton, Illinois 62341

MOVIES AND DOCUMENTARIES

Tales from the Hive (1998)
See WWW.PBS.ORG/WGBH/NOVA/BEES/

Taking the Bugs for a Ride (2006)
See WWW.HACKENBERGAPIARIES.COM

PollenNation (2007)
See WWW.POLLENNATIONTHEMOVIE.COM

WEBSITES TO EXPLORE

WWW.POLLINATOR.ORG
This website includes pollinator-friendly planting guides for every region in the United States, a pollinator curriculum for students in grades three through five, and lots of information on organizations and projects designed to support honey bees and other natural pollinators.

WWW.HELPTHEHONEYBEES.COM
Häagen-Dazs has created this website to help educate the world about honey bees and their crucial role in the production of, among other things, ice cream; the site includes a free, downloadable educational booklet on honey bees.

WWW.XERCES.ORG
The Xerces Society works to conserve all invertebrate species, including honey bees. Their website is a treasure trove of useful information, including downloadable fact sheets that will help you plant a bee-friendly garden.

MAAREC.CAS.PSU.EDU
The website of the Mid-Atlantic Apiculture Research and Extension Consortium contains a wealth of historical information on colony collapse disorder, including background information, dated research updates, surveys, and news.

ACKNOWLEDGMENTS

Creating this book was an incredible adventure, and I owe a debt of gratitude to the many people who helped make it possible. Hive detectives Dave Hackenberg, Dennis vanEngelsdorp, Jeff Pettis, Diana Cox-Foster, and Maryann Frazier—as well as their laboratory and field colleagues—generously shared their work and their time. Mary Duane shared her passion for beekeeping; Gus Skamarycz shared his steady hand (and three perfectly placed stings!); Don and Jean Holm shared their beehives; and the Worcester County Beekeepers Association shared all the bee knowledge and expertise this wannabee asked for. Special thanks to my friend Linda Miller, who sent the newspaper clipping that got me started, and to Dewey Caron and Ken Warchol, who diligently reviewed the manuscript for technical accuracy. Writers Liza Martz, Eric Luper, Kate Messner, Linda Urban, and Dawn Lussier, agent Ken Wright, and editor Erica Zappy shared wisdom and encouragement in equal measure: I am lucky to work with each of them. Photographer Ellen Harasimowicz shared much of the journey and captured its highlights in stunning photographs; this book represents the beginning of what I hope will be a long and fruitful partnership between us. Designer Cara Llewellyn took my words and Ellen's images and turned them into an irresistible reading experience; well done, Cara, and thank you! Special thanks to my husband, Gerry, and our children, Sam, Ben, and Cat, who have learned more about bees these last couple years than perhaps they wanted to know. I appreciate their patience and love them dearly!

SELECT REFERENCES

Barrionuevo, Alexei. "Honeybees Vanish, Leaving Keepers in Peril." *New York Times,* February 27, 2007.

Caron, Dewey. *Honey Bee Biology and Beekeeping.* Connecticut: Wicwas Press, 1999.

Committee on the Status of Pollinators in North America, National Research Council. *Status of Pollinators in North America.* Washington D.C.: National Academies Press, 2007.

Cox-Foster, Diana, et al. "A Metagenomic Survey of Microbes in Honey Bee Colony Collapse Disorder." *Science* 318 (2007): 283-87.

Evans, Arthur V., editor. *Field Guide to Insects and Spiders of North America.* New York: Sterling Publishing Company, 2007.

Flottum, Kim. "We're All We've Got." *Bee Culture,* June 2008, p. 10.

Frazier, Maryann, Chris Mullin, Jim Frazier, and Sara Ashcroft. "What Have Pesticides Got to Do with It?" *American Bee Journal* 148 (2008): 521–23.

Henderson, Colin, Larry Tarver, David Plummer, and Robert Seccomb. "U.S. National Bee Colony Loss Survey: Preliminary Findings with Respect to Colony Collapse Disorder (CCD)." *American Bee Journal* 147 (2007): 381–84.

Jacobsen, Rowan. *Fruitless Fall.* New York: Bloomsbury, 2008.

Review of Colony Collapse Disorder in Honey Bee Colonies Across the United States. Hearing before the Subcommittee on Horticulture and Organic Agriculture of the Committee on Agriculture, House of Representatives. March 29, 2007. Transcript serial no. 110-07.

vanEngelsdorp, Dennis, Diana Cox-Foster, Maryann Frazier, and Nancy Ostiguy. "Fall-Dwindle Disease: Investigations into the Causes of Sudden and Alarming Colony Losses Experienced by Beekeepers in the Fall of 2006 Preliminary Report: First Revision." Published on MAAREC website, 2006.

vanEngelsdorp, Dennis, Robyn Underwood, Dewey Caron, and Jerry Hayes, Jr. "An Estimate of Managed Colony Losses in the Winter of 2006–2007: A Report Commissioned by the Apiary Inspectors of America." *American Bee Journal* 147 (2007) 599–603.

Research Update

"Tracking CCD continues to be complex. Despite several claims, we still don't know the cause."

—Jeff Pettis, Research Leader, U.S. Department of Agriculture

In the two years since this book was published, honey bee colonies have continued to collapse. The hive detectives—Dennis, Jeff, Diana, Maryann, and their many colleagues—are still searching for the reasons why. Most of these experts now agree on two things:

1. Not all the honey bee colony losses recorded over the past five years can be attributed to colony collapse disorder.

2. The many stress factors described in this book—hive pests (mites, Nosema, etc.), viruses, pesticides, poor nutrition, and hive management—can each play a role in colony loss.

What is harder for scientists and beekeepers to agree on is exactly what combination of stress factors leads to the strange condition we call CCD.

Recently Jeff and Dennis conducted experiments in which they treated honey bee colonies with very small amounts of a neonicotinoid pesticide (see page 43) and then exposed young bees from these colonies to the gut parasite Nosema (see page 31). Their results showed that honey bees from the pesticide-exposed colonies developed much stronger Nosema infections. These results suggest that exposure to small amounts of pesticide, even levels that don't kill honey bees outright, can have disastrous consequences on the future of a colony. They also support the notion that overall colony health is defined by stress factors in combination.

No matter what is causing CCD, the process of trying to understand it has shed light on the plight of honey bees and other pollinators. This is a good thing. The most recent survey of U.S. beekeepers indicates that fewer honey bee colonies were lost in 2011-12 than in the five years prior. It's too soon to know if this trend will continue, but the hope is that things the hive detectives have learned about honey

bees and honey bee health while investigating the CCD crisis—and the changes in beekeeping and land management this knowledge has inspired—is making the world a little safer for honey bees.

Research Update References:

Pettis et al. "Pesticide Exposure in Honey Bees Results in Increased Levels of the Gut Pathogen Nosema." <u>Naturwissenschaften</u> 99 (2012): 153–58.

Spivak et al. "The Plight of the Bees." <u>Environmental Science & Technology</u> 45 (2011): 34–38.

USDA Press Release, May 31, 2012, www.ars.usda.gov/is/pr/2012/120531.htm.

INDEX

Page numbers in **bold** type refer to photos and their captions.

SCIENTISTS IN THE FIELD
Where Science Meets Adventure

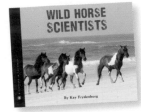

Check out these titles to meet more scientists who are out in the field—and contributing every day to our knowledge of the world around us:

Looking for even more adventure? Craving updates on the work of your favorite scientists, as well as in-depth video footage, audio, photography, and more? Then visit the new Scientists in the Field website!

www.sciencemeetsadventure.com